Novena For The Relief Of The Poor Souls In Purgatory

by Fr. J. F. Durin, A Missionary Of The Sacred Heart

"He that stoppeth his ear against the cry of the poor, shall also cry himself and shall not be heard." (Prov. XXI, 13.)

Table of Contents

To The Pious Reader..5

Preparatory Prayer...7

De Profundis (Psalm 129) 8

First Day: Existence of Purgatory 9

Second Day: Pains of Purgatory 11

Third Day: The Pain of Loss...13

Fourth Day: The Pain of Sense 15

The Fifth Day: Duration of Purgatory 17

The Sixth Day: Obligation of Assisting the "Poor Souls." 19

The Seventh Day: Cruelty of Those Who Abandon the "Poor Souls." 21

The Eighth Day: The Communion of Saints 23

The Ninth Day: Benefit of the Devotion to the "Poor Souls." 25

Saint Alphonsus on Our Duty to the Poor Souls.........................27

Other Books From Christ the King Library.................................32

To The Pious Reader

We present this small treatise to pious persons, entreating them to peruse it. Long ago the Holy Ghost said: "It is a holy and wholesome thing to pray for the dead, that they may be loosed from their sins." (II Macabees 12:46) Our Lord shed tears in seeing the tomb of Lazarus, and the Church, well acquainted with the feelings of her Divine Founder, is incessently recommending charity for the Souls suffering in Purgatory. One of her eminent doctors, St. Thomas of Aquinas, has said that: "Of all prayers, the most meritorious, the most acceptable to God are prayers for the dead, because they imply all the works of charity, both corporal and spiritual."

But there are many people unconscious of the fact that charity for the "Poor Souls" is profitable to the living as well as to the dead. It is the teaching of the most learned theologians, viz: St. Alphonsus Ligori, Sylvius, Robert Bellarmine, Bonacina, and Suarez. "It is true," says St. Alphonsus, "they are unable to pray or merit anything for themselves, yet, when they pray for others, they are heard by God." Let us refer to Bellarmine: "The Souls in Purgatory," says he, "can pray for those, who address to them their petitions, and obtain from God help, forgiveness, assistance against temptations, and, all favors, both temporal and spiritual, which they may need."

Many Saints have experienced this wonderful assistance. St. Catherine of Bologna assured her Sisters that: "She obtained many favors by the prayers of the holy Souls in Purgatory, which she had asked in vain, through the intercession of the Saints." St. Theresa affirms that: "She always obtained the favors which she asked from God, through the intercession of the Poor Souls." We read also in the book of St. Bridget's Revelations that: "Being one day conducted by an Angel into Purgatory, she heard a soul say: "Oh Lord, vouchsafe to reward those who assist us! Return hundredfold blessings to those who help us and introduce us into the light of Heaven." St. Leonard of Port Maurice emphatically affirms that: "The blessed Souls, delivered by our prayers, will come down from Heaven to assist us in our temporal and spiritual affairs." The Venerable Cure d' Ars, replying to a priest said: "If one knew what we may obtain from God by the intercession of the Poor Souls, they would not be so much abandoned. Let us pray a great deal for them, they will pray for us."

Blessed Margaret Mary Alacoque had a special devotion for the Souls in Purgatory and has often accepted the charge of suffering for them. "Would that you knew," she said, "how my soul was replenished with joy, when speaking to those Souls, and seeing them immersed in glory as in a deep ocean. As I requested them to pray for you, they replied: "An ungrateful soul is not to be found in Heaven!" No, we cannot be deceived! If we have an ardent charity, a sincere piety, a true devotedness for the Poor Souls, we will be favored with their protection.

Let us try it! When we are in trouble, when we long for a favor, let us perform some pious or charitable work for the relief of the "Poor Souls." They will be grateful, they will plead for us, and present our requests to the Eternal Father, Who loves them.

May God bless this humble work! May He deign to enkindle generous hearts with zeal for the "Poor Souls."

"Blessed are the merciful: for they shall obtain mercy." (Matt., V., 7.)

Preparatory Prayer

(To be said every day of the novena.)

Act of Faith: My God, I believe in Thee, because Thou art Truth itself; I firmly believe the truths revealed to the Church.

Act of Hope: My God, I hope in Thee, because Thou art infinitely good.

Act of Charity: My God, I love Thee with all my heart, and above all things, because Thou are infinitely perfect; and I love my neighbor as myself, for the love of Thee.

De Profundis (Psalm 129)

(To be said every day of the novena.)

Out of the depths I have cried to Thee, O Lord: Lord hear my voice.

Let Thy ears be attentive to the voice of my supplication.

If Thou, O Lord, wilt mark iniquities; Lord, who shall stand it?

For with Thee there is merciful forgiveness: and by reason of Thy law,

I have waited for Thee, O Lord.

My soul hath relied on His word: my soul hath hoped in the Lord.

From the morning-watch even until night, let Israel hope in the Lord.

Because with the Lord there is mercy: and with Him plentiful redemption.

And He shall redeem Israel from all his iniquities.

V. Eternal rest give unto them. O Lord.

R. And let perpetual light shine upon them.

V. From the gate of Hell.

R. Deliver their souls, O Lord.

V. May they rest in peace.

R. Amen.

V. Lord, hear my prayer.

R. And let my cry come unto Thee.

V. The Lord be with you.

R. And with Thy Spirit.

Let us pray: O God, the Creator and Redeemer of all the faithful, we beseech Thee to grant to the Souls of Thy servants the remission of their sins, so that by our prayers they may obtain pardon for which they long. O Lord, Who livest and reignest, world without end. Amen.

May they rest in peace. Amen.

First Day: Existence of Purgatory

Say Preparatory Prayer

Meditation: There is a place for the purification of Souls which, after death, are yet stained with venial sins, or have not yet entirely satisfied for their pardoned sins. The Holy Catholic Church teaches it. I believe it firmly. By the light of the flames of Purgatory, I understand better Thy holiness, Thy Justice, Thy Mercy, O my God! "Who shall ascend into the mountain of the Lord? or who shall stand in His Holy Place? The innocent in hands, and clean of heart." (Ps. 23.) "There shall not enter into Heaven anything defiled." (Apoc. 21.) For Thou art Holy! Holy! Holy! O Lord, inspire my soul with the horror of sin! Grant me the grace to atone for my faults here below! Thou art just, O Lord, and Thy judgments are right. Who will dare to say: "Do not condemn me: tell me why Thou judgest me so?" (Job, X, 2.) "To Thee only have I sinned, and have done evil before Thee." (Ps. 50, 6.) I have deserved eternal punishment, but Thy mercy will follow me---it will follow me into the depth of death, and I will be spared.

Oh, Purgatory! where reigns Hope! There I will say with the Prophet: "When I was in distress Thou hast enlarged me!" (Ps. IV., 1.) If there were no Purgatory, where would so many lazy, negligent, unmortified souls go? "Blessed be the God and Father of our Lord Jesus Christ, the Father of mercies, and the God of all comfort, Who comforteth us in all our tribulation." (II Cor. 1., 3., 4.)

Practice: To pray the Divine Heart of Jesus that He deign to enkindle many souls with an ardent charity for the Souls in Purgatory.

Resolution: Every day of my life I will pray or do some good work for the "Poor Souls."

Example: It is related in the Acts of St. Perpetua, Martyr, that, being thrown into prison, she was favored with a vision. She saw her young brother, Dinocrates, in a dark place. He was surrounded by flames, thirsty, his face was ugly, pale, covered with an ulcer, which caused his death, when seven years old. She prayed fervently for him during seven days, and then he appeared to her in a very different condition. He was bright, clothed with a beautiful white dress, and there was no ulcer on his face. She understod that he had been delivered.

Prayer: De Profundis

Let us pray for our departed parents: O God, Who has commanded us to honor our Father and Mother, have pity on them, deliver them from the pains which they have deserved, and grant that I may see them in the glory of Heaven. Through our Lord Jesus Christ. Amen.

V. Eternal rest give unto them, O Lord.

R. And let perpetual light shine upon them.

V. May they rest in peace.

R. Amen.

Second Day: Pains of Purgatory

Say Preparatory Prayer

Meditation: Let us go with our Guardian Angel to Purgatory, to that place where the Divine Justice purifies Souls before they are admitted into Heaven.

There we will meet again our parents and our friends. Had this devotion no other advantage than that of reminding us of our departed ones, we should be grateful to God for such a consolation.

Oh, my father! Oh, my mother! Oh, brothers! Oh, sisters! Oh, friends! I had forgotten you! What do you suffer, beloved Souls? What shall I do to deliver you?

Our pains, they reply, are beyond description. When separated from our body, we saw the face of God, our Supreme Good, the Infinite Perfection. Then would we rush into His bosom, but we were driven back by His Justice, we were banished! Oh, no! on earth below you will never understand our pain, our grief, because we are separated from God! Your troubles, your sorrows, are the mere shadow of our affliction. But we suffer through our fault. If we would return to our former place on earth, we would be glad to accept the hardest mortification in exchange for Purgatory. "Have pity on me, have pity on me, at least you my friends, because the hand of the Lord hath touched me!" (Job. 19, 21.) Appease the Divine Justice with your good works, pay our debts, hasten the day when we shall enter into Heaven, and then we will return our gratitude forever.

Practice: Encourage all the works established for the relief of the Souls in Purgatory.

Resolution: At night, in the examination of conscience, I will question myself: What have you done today for the relief of Poor Souls?

Example: The soul of a pious lady, deceased at Luxemburg, appeared on All Saints' Day to a young girl of great piety, to beg the assistance of her prayers. When the latter was going to church, when approaching the holy rails, she was followed by the soul. Outside the church it could not be seen. As the young girl inquired the reason for it, she was answered: "You cannot understand how painful it is to be away from God. I am attracted to God by impetuous transports, by intolerable anxiety, and I am condemned to live far away from Him. My sorrow is so intense, that the ardor of fire, which surrounds me, is a lesser suffering. To soothe my pain, God, in His mercy, has allowed me to come into this church, and to adore Him, veiled under the Host, until I might see Him face to face in Heaven." She entreated the young girl to pray for her deliverance. It was done with so much fervor, that, on the 10th of December, the soul appeared, as bright as the sun, going to Heaven.

Prayer: De Profundis

Let us pray for our benefactors and friends: O God, Who bestowest forgiveness and salvation, we address Thy clemency that, through the intercession of the blessed Virgin Mary and of all the Saints, the Souls of our departed brethren, relatives and benefactors, may be admitted into the eternal glory. Through our Lord Jesus Christ. Amen.

V. Eternal rest give unto them, O Lord.

R. And let perpetual light shine upon them.

V. May they rest in peace.

R. Amen.

Third Day: The Pain of Loss

Say Preparatory Prayer

Meditation: During the long captivity, God's people, sitting on the shores of the Euphrates, moaned and cried in remembering Sion. So the Souls in Purgatory, plaintive and doleful, long for the joys of the heavenly mansion. They have had a glimpse of its glory and happiness, but because they were too much attached to earthly pleasures, they will be deprived, perhaps for a long time, of the celestial joys. They remember all the negligence of their former life, which now obstructs their way to Heaven. What sorrows! what remorses! because they have preferred a moment of pleasure to the enjoyment of Heaven. Then the poor, desolate Souls accuse themselves, saying with the Prophet: "I know my iniquity, and my sin is always before me." (Ps. 50, 5)

Since God has granted us the power of paying the debts of the "Poor Souls" with our works, let us appreciate this immense privilege. A noble heart should be delighted in relieving the poor, in consoling the afflicted, in bringing peace and happiness to those who suffer. Such is the privilege of those who assist the Souls suffering in Purgatory, because they deliver them from the hardest captivity and they open to them the gates of Heaven.

Moreover our charitable deeds for the "Poor Souls" will secure for us the gratitude of God Himself. "When," said our Lord to His holy servant Gertrude, "a Soul is liberated by your prayers, I accept it, as if I had been Myself liberated from captivity, and I will assuredly reward you according to the abundance of My mercy."

Practice: Perform today an act of mortification or obedience for the relief of the "Poor Souls."

Resolution: Be faithful in little things. Everything is great which is done for the Glory of God.

Example: At the close of September, 1870, there died at GH, France, a banker, renowned for his piety and his charity. By Divine permission his Soul appeared to his daughter, a member of a sisterhood in Belgium, to implore the assistance of her prayers. At first he was seen surrounded by flames, saying: "Have pity on your father, my child! If Purgatory were known, everyone would strive to escape its torments." Sometimes he would loudly complain: "I thirst! I thirst!"

Fervent prayers were offered for him at the convent, and he appeared again, enveloped in a dark cloud, but free from fire. He said to his daughter: "It seems that I am here during a century. My great suffering now is the thirst for the Vision of God and the enjoyment of His presence. I rush to Him and I am incessantly repulsed into the abyss because I have not yet paid all my debt to the Divine Justice."

Prayers were continued and on Christmas night he was seen in a halo of light, and addressing his daughter, said: "My pains are over. I owe this favor to the prayers offered for me. I come to thank you and your community. I will not forget you in Heaven."

Prayer: De Profundis

Let us pray for Bishops and Priests deceased: O God, Who has deigned to raise to the pontifical or sacerdotal dignity Thy servants N. N., grant us the grace of enjoying with them eternal felicity. Through our Lord Jesus Christ. Amen.

V. Eternal rest give unto them, O Lord.

R. And let perpetual light shine upon them.

V. May they rest in peace.

R. Amen.

Fourth Day: The Pain of Sense

Say Preparatory Prayer

Meditation: The pain of loss, the deprivation of the Vision of God, constitutes the supreme suffering in Purgatory. To this suffering of deprivation other sufferings of a positive nature are added. These are conditioned by the number and gravity of the sins which call for expiation and we have every reason to conceive of them as alike terrible and prolonged. Though the Church has not pronounced any decision on this point, it is the opinion of its doctors that the Souls in Purgatory are tormented by fire which penetrates them and burns them as gold in the crucible (Prov. 17, 3) until it has reduced them to such a degree of purity, that they may be worthy to appear before God.

When a fire is raging, everybody is excited. The people rush to the spot and everyone tries to save those who are already surrounded by the terrible element. Why are we unmoved at the sight of so many Souls who are tormented in the fire of Purgatory and who claim our assistance? Let us not abandon them.

Practice: Let us pray our Lord today to apply the merit of His death on the Cross to the Souls in Purgatory.

Resolution: I will observe the abstinence and fast prescribed by the Church, unless prevented by sickness.

Example: Two Spanish monks, bound together by a long and warm friendship, agreed that: if God would allow it, the one who should die first, would appear to the other to make known his condition in the other world. Some time later, one of them died, and appeared to his friend, saying: "I am saved, but condemned to suffer in Purgatory. It is impossible to describe such torments. Will you allow me to give you a sensible demonstration?" Then he placed his hand on the table and imprinted on it a mark as deep as if it had been made by a red hot iron. This table was preserved at Zamora (Spain) up to within the last century.

Prayer: De Profundis

Let us pray for a deceased man: Hear, O Lord, the prayers which we address to Thy mercy, and grant us that the soul of Thy servant N.N., which is gone into another world, be received into the abode of light and happiness to enjoy the felicity of the Saints. Through our Lord Jesus Christ. Amen.

V. Eternal rest give unto them, O Lord.
R. And let perpetual light shine upon them.
V. May they rest in peace.
R. Amen.

The Fifth Day: Duration of Purgatory

Say Preparatory Prayer

Meditation: How long do the pains last in Purgatory? Nobody knows. God has allowed some Souls to appear to their friends and benefactors to announce their departure for Heaven, but it seldom happened, and we cannot draw any conclusion from such cases. The period of confinement in Purgatory is probably much longer than we are inclined to think. Oh! how much combustible matter---how many imperfections, venial sins and temporal punishments due to mortal and venial sins---do you think they took with them to be cancelled in the flames of Purgatory? Centuries may pass until Divine Justice is satisfied and the Poor Soul is so purified as to be admitted to the Vision of God. The Venerable Bede relates that it was revealed to Drithelm, a great servant of God, that the Souls of those who spend their whole lives in the state of mortal sin, and are converted only on their death bed, are doomed to suffer the pains of Purgatory to the day of Last Judgment. Father Faber, commenting on this subject, says very justly: "We are not to leave off too soon praying for our parents, friends or relatives, imagining with a foolish and unenlightened esteem for the holiness of their lives, that they are freed from Purgatory much sooner than they really are!"

Let us consider the purity which is necessary to a soul, before being admitted into the presence of God! Let us remember the multitude of our venial sins, and see what light penance we have done for them. On the Day of Judgment the book of our deeds will be opened, and then we will be obliged to pay the last farthing. How guilty we are in abandoning so easily the Souls who need our assistance so much! The Saints are wiser. St. Monica, the mother of St. Augustine, was dead for twenty years, and she was still remembered by her son in the Holy Sacrifice. St. Ambrose promised solemnly and publicly to pray, during his entire life, for the soul of Theodosius the Great.

And supposing that we had delivered the Souls of our relatives and friends, have we emptied the prison of Purgatory?

How many poor, abandoned Souls linger in such horrible pains, imploring the assistance of some charitable heart. Cardinal Belllarmine has affirmed that: "Some Souls would suffer in Purgatory till the Day of Judgment, if they were not relieved by the prayer of the Church."

Therefore, he authorizes the foundation of Masses to be said in perpetuity.

Practice: Would it not be a holy thought to form, among relatives and friends, an association of seven members, so that each would employ a day of the week for the relief of the "Poor Souls."

Resolution: Each time I hear the clock strike, I will say:

V. Eternal rest give unto them, O Lord.

R. And let perpetual light shine upon them.

(50 days each time for saying this V. and R., applicable only to the dead. Leo XIII Br., March 22, 1902.)

Example: Sister Denis, one of the first members of the order of the Visitation, was a zealous promoter of the devotion of the "Poor Souls." It was revealed to her that a prince, one of her relatives, had been condemned to suffer in Purgatory until the Day of Judgment. She offered herself as a victim for the relief of this soul. On her death-bed she said to the mother-superior that she had obtained for the poor soul the remittance of some hours of his pain. As the superior wondered at this fact, she replied: "O Mother, time in Purgatory is not counted as on earth; years passed here in sorrow, in poverty, in sickness, in suffering, are nothing, if we compare them with one hour in Purgatory!"

Prayer: De Profundis

Let us pray for a deceased woman: We humbly request Thee, O Lord, to grant mercy to the soul of Thy Servant, N. N., in order that, being delivered from the contagion of sin, she may enter into eternal salvation. Through our Lord Jesus Christ. Amen.

V. Eternal rest give unto them, O Lord.

R. And let perpetual light shine upon them.

V. May they rest in peace.

R. Amen.

The Sixth Day: Obligation of Assisting the "Poor Souls."

Say Preparatory Prayer

Meditation: The Souls in Purgatory cannot help themselves; they are unable to shorten their captivity. This reason alone should urge us to come to their assistance.

After death there is no more place for mercy, the time for justice commences. The soul is no longer free to choose between good and evil, therefore she cannot obtain any merit and her sufferings are accounted only as a payment for her debts. Alas! to be condemned to such sufferings, to be afflicted perhaps during centuries! How bad it is for those "Poor Souls!"

Could we see an unfortunate man, lying on the road, wounded, bleeding and would we pass and abandon him! We hold the key of a prison, crowded with prisoners; they crave for liberty and shall we leave them in their pitiable situation! So we have received from the mercy of God the privilege of liberating the Souls detained in Purgatory. We may say that we are the Providence of the dead; we, and we alone, may open the gates of Heaven to the Souls who are longing for their deliverance. It is the teaching of the Church, that the prayer of the living can be applied to the Souls in Purgatory. As your prayers ascend to Heaven, graces come down as a refreshing shower, bringing to the Souls forgiveness, liberty, and glory. The supplications of Mary and Martha obtained the resurrection of Lazarus. Let us address our prayers to the heart of Jesus, and we will deliver from their pains our dear departed ones. Shall we not be guilty if we do not employ our credit in favor of the unfortunate prisoners in Purgatory?

Practice: St. John Chrysostom recommended to every Christian family that they have a box at some convenient place in the house and that they put into it pennies, which will be used to have Masses said for the "Poor Souls."

Resolution: Pray today for the most abandoned Souls.

Example: At the Benedictine monasteries, when one of the monks died, his ordinary meals are distributed among the poor during thirty days. In the year 830, when a terrible plague was raging, many religious died. The abbot Rabanun Maurus gave the order to distribute the alms, according to the ancient usage, but the procurator did not obey. One night the stingy monk, having been delayed by his work, to shorten his way to his cell, passed through the Chapter room. There he was surrounded by all the monks, recently dead, who whipped him, leaving him half dead on the floor. Early the next morning he was found by the religious, who were going to the chapel. He related the event, made his confession, received the last rites and died two days afterwards.

Prayer: De Profundis

Let us pray: We humbly beseech Thee, O Lord, to release the Souls of Thy Servants, in order that they may obtain the glory of the resurrection and that they may be joined to the Saints and elect in Heaven. Through our Lord Jesus Christ. Amen.

V. Eternal rest give unto them, O Lord.

R. And let perpetual light shine upon them.

V. May they rest in peace.

R. Amen.

The Seventh Day: Cruelty of Those Who Abandon the "Poor Souls."

Say Preparatory Prayer

Meditation: Our Lord reproved the cruelty of the rich man, who refused even the crumbs of his table to poor Lazarus. while he himself was feasting sumptuously every day. Are they not imitating the wicked rich, who stand unmoved, seeing the sufferings of the "Poor Souls?" Those unfortunates, who appeal to our compassion, are not strangers. Among them there are our parents, our benefactors, our friends. Not long ago, they were living among us in the same house. We bear their names, we inherited their lands; and we forgot them! We abandon them! They may say with Job: "My kinsmen have forsaken me, and they that knew me have forgotten me. They that dwell in my house, and my maid-servants, have counted me as a stranger, and I have been like an alien in their eyes." (Job 19, 15) To forget the dead is a crime. Solemn promises were made at the death-bed. A child has said to his father and to his mother dying: I will not forget you! But where is the sign of this remembrance? Does it pray for them? Perhaps a vague, shadowy remembrance of the departed comes to its mind, but where is the profit to the "Poor Souls?" Useless and vain compassion! Empty love! Where are the works, alms, and holy Masses to assist, to relieve, to deliver the "Poor Souls?" Those who forget them will also be abandoned! "With what measure you mete, it shall be measured to you again." (St. Matt. 7, 22)

Practice: After the Evening Angelus say: Our Father and Hail Mary, once; or the De Profundis, as a daily tribute to the "Poor Souls."

Resolution: I will endeavor to propagate devotion to the "Poor Souls."

Example: A poor servant-girl had the pious custom of having a Mass said every month for the Souls in Purgatory, and she prayed especially for the Soul that was nearest to Heaven. After a long, protracted illness, she was leaving the hospital and setting out in search of a position. On her way she passed a church and, remembering that her monthly Mass had not been said, she entered the sacristy, requesting the priest to say this Mass. When she left the church a young man came up to her. He was tall and pale, and of a noble demeanor. "My good girl," he said, "I think you are looking for a position." "Yes," said the girl, somewhat surprised. "Well," said the young man, "if you go to Mrs. N. (here he named the street and number), I think you will find a good place;" and suddenly he disappeared among the crowd of passersby. The girl went, found the house, was introduced, and presented her petition. "But," said the lady of the house, "who could have sent you here? Nobody knows that I need a servant." Suddenly the girl, looking at the wall, noticed a portrait. "Look here, madam," said she, pointing to the picture, "that is the exact likeness of the man who told me to come here." At these words the old lady turned pale. "Ah!" said she, "that is the portrait of my son, who died two years ago. You shall henceforward remain with me, not as a servant-girl, but as my daughter, and we will always pray together for the "Poor Souls" in Purgatory."

Prayer: De Profundis

Let us pray: May our prayers be profitable, O Lord, to the Souls of Thy servants, that being absolved from their sins, they may have a share in the fruits of redemption. Through Our Lord Jesus Christ. Amen.

V. Eternal rest give unto them, O Lord.

R. And let perpetual light shine upon them.

V. May they rest in peace.

R. Amen.

The Eighth Day: The Communion of Saints

Say Preparatory Prayer

Meditation: How grand and consoling is the doctrine of the Communion of Saints! While we, in this world, are struggling for the celestial crown, and assist our brethren in Purgatory, we are protected by those who are triumphing in Heaven. We form, in reality, but one and the same family here below, in Purgatory, and in Heaven. If a member of our body is suffering, all other members come to its assistance. God loves the Souls in Purgatory as His dear spouses. He would open to them the gates of Heaven, but there are barriers. Let us present to His justice our prayers, our good works, and the obstruction will be removed; God will be satisfied.

It is often an obligation of justice to pray for the Poor Souls, but it is always a duty imposed by charity and by the compassion which we owe to one another.

There are in Purgatory Souls abandoned even by their parents and their friends, and for whom no one cares. Forgotten is their life, no thinking of it anymore; forgotten is their name; forgotten is their grave, which is visited no more; forgotten is their Soul, which is lingering in the fire of Purgatory. How their pain is increased by such neglect; They may say with the Prophet: "I am forgotten as one dead from the heart. I am become as a vessel that is destroyed." (Ps. 30, 30.)

Practice: Let us pray often and do some good works for the most abandoned Souls. Let us be to them like a father, a mother, a sister, a friend.

Resolution: To offer the abandonment of our Lord Jesus, in His passion, for the most abandoned Souls.

Example: Catherine of Cortona was hardly eight years old when her father died. One day he appeared to her, wrapt in fire. "My daughter," said he, "I will be plunged in fire till you have done penance for me." Then the child, with a rare courage, decided to practice the hardest mortifications, in order to pay the spiritual debts of her father. She succeeded. Her father appeared again, as bright as a Saint, saying: "God has accepted your suffrages and your satisfactory works, my daughter. 1 am going to enjoy eternal happiness. Do not cease to offer yourself as a victim for the salvation of Suffering Souls. This is the will of God."

Prayer: De Profundis

Let us pray for those who rest in the cemetery: O God, by whose mercy the Souls of the departed rest in peace, we beseech Thee to grant to Thy servants, and to all who rest in the Lord, the forgiveness of their sins, and life everlasting. Through our Lord Jesus Christ. Amen.

V. Eternal rest give unto them, O Lord.

R. And let perpetual light shine upon them.

V. May they rest in peace.

R. Amen.

The Ninth Day: Benefit of the Devotion to the "Poor Souls."

Say Preparatory Prayer

Meditation: This Novena is coming to a close. Do we understand the benefits and the consolation derived from devotion to the holy Souls? Do we need stronger motives to increase our zeal? Then let us consider that: Nothing is more glorious to God, nothing gives more honor to His Holy Name, nothing rejoices His Heart more, nothing is more pleasing to Him than charity for the "Poor Souls."

To open Heaven to the Poor Souls is to praise and glorify God, the number of hearts that love Him. "Such a work," says Bourdaloue, "is an apostolate more noble, more meritorious than the conversion of sinners, and even of heathens."

How we will please the Heart of Jesus, Who loves the Souls redeemed by His Precious Blood! He would willingly come into this world again and offer Himself for their deliverance; but all justice must be accomplished, and the debts of the Souls must be paid. Therefore, He has inspired His Church with the practice of praying for the dead every time the Holy Sacrifice is offered.

The Blessed Virgin is the Queen of Purgatory and will be highly gratified when we contribute to the relief of the "Poor Souls."

St. Joseph, the patron of a happy death, will also present our requests to the Lord, who has been called His Son. He will repay us generously if we come to the rescue of the suffering Souls.

What joy among the Saints in Heaven when they will see another elect---a Soul coming out of Purgatory! Her Guardian Angel, the Holy Patron, will welcome and congratulate her! It will be a great joy in Heaven. The Saints know the benefactors of the "Poor Souls," and they will, in return, protect them.

We have already said that the Saints in Purgatory will remember their benefactors. No, they cannot forget them! They will attentively provide for them in needs both temporal and spiritual. They will protect us and defend us in troubles, in dangers, in temptations. On our death-bed they will surround us. At the tribunal of God they will be our advocates; and, if we are cast into Purgatory, they will come to visit us, to console us, until the day of our entrance into a glorious eternity.

Practice: Give alms to the poor; insure your soul with prayers and good deeds against the fire of Purgatory. Money will be useless at the hour of death, but your good works will follow you.

Resolution: I will never miss the opportunity of assisting the "Poor Souls."

Example: A pious lady was praying for the recovery of her health. She had exhausted every means and made novenas after novenas to the Blessed Virgin Mary, to St. Joseph, etc., without success. But she was advised to commence novenas for the relief of the "Poor Souls" in Purgatory. She did so and entirely recovered. She was accustomed to say: "All that I ask through the intercession of the "Poor Souls" I obtain easily. With them I am never discouraged, and I hope against hope."

Prayer: De Profundis

Let us pray for all the faithful departed: O God, Creator and Redeemer of all men, we beseech Thee to grant to the Souls of Thy servants the remission of their sins, so that by our prayers they may obtain the indulgence for which they long. O Lord, Who reigns and lives, world without end. Amen.

V. Eternal rest give unto them, O Lord.

R. And let perpetual light shine upon them.

V. May they rest in peace.

R. Amen.

Saint Alphonsus on Our Duty to the Poor Souls

Is it good to invoke the souls in purgatory?

Again, it is disputed whether there is any use in recommending one's self to the souls in purgatory. Some say that the souls in that state cannot pray for us; and these rely on the authority of St. Thomas, who says that those souls, while they are being purified by pain, are inferior to us, and therefore 'are not in a state to pray for us, but rather require our prayers.' But many other Doctors, as Bellarmine, Sylvius, Cardinal Gotti, Lessius, Medina and others affirm with great probability, that we should piously believe that God manifests our prayer to those holy souls in order that they may pray for us; and that so the charitable interchange of mutual prayer may be kept up between them and us. Nor do St. Thomas' words present much difficulty; for, as Sylvius and Gotti say, it is one thing not to be in a state to pray, another not to be able to pray. It is true that those souls are not in a state to pray, because, as St. Thomas says, while suffering they are inferior to us, and rather require our prayers; nevertheless, in this state they are well able to pray, as they are friends of God. If a father keeps a son whom he tenderly loves in confinement for some fault; if the son then is not in a state to pray for himself, is that any reason why he cannot pray for others? and may he not expect to obtain what he asks, knowing, as he does, his father's affection for him? So the souls in purgatory, being beloved by God, and confirmed in grace, have absolutely no impediment to prevent them from praying for us. Still the Church does not invoke them, or implore their intercession, because ordinarily they have no cognizance of our prayers. But we may piously believe that God makes our prayers known to them; and then they, full of charity as they are, most assuredly do not omit to pray for us. St. Catharine of Bologna, whenever she desired any favour, had recourse to the souls in purgatory, and was immediately heard. She even testified that by the intercession of the souls in purgatory she had obtained many graces which she had not been able to obtain by the intercession of the saints.

Our duty to pray for the souls in purgatory.

Here let me make a digression in favour of those holy souls. If we desire the aid of their prayers, it is but fair that we should mind to aid them with our prayers and good works. I said it is fair, but I should have said it is a Christian duty; for charity obliges us to succour our neighbour when he requires our aid, and we can help him without grievous inconvenience. Now it is certain that amongst our neighbours are to be reckoned the souls in purgatory, who, although no longer living in this world, yet have not left the communion of saints. 'The souls of the pious dead,' says St. Augustine, 'are not separated from the Church,' and St. Thomas says more to our purpose, that the charity which is due to the dead who died in the grace of God is only an extension of the same charity which we owe to our neighbour while living: 'Charity, which is the bond which unites the members of the Church, extends not only to the living, but also to the dead who die in charity.' Therefore, we ought to succour, according to our ability, those holy souls as our neighbours; and as their necessities are greater than those of our other neighbours, our duty to succour them seems also to be greater.

But now, what are the necessities of those holy prisoners? It is certain that their pains are immense. The fire that tortures them, says St. Augustine, is more excruciating than any pain that man can endure in this life: That fire will be more painful than anything that man can suffer in this life.' St. Thomas thinks the same, and supposes it to be identical with the fire of hell: 'The damned are tormented and the elect purified in the same fire.' And this only relates to the pains of sense. But the pain of loss (that is, the privation of the sight of God), which those holy souls suffer, is much greater; because not only their natural affection, but also the supernatural love of God, wherewith they burn, draws them with such violence to be united with their Sovereign Good, that when they see the barrier which their sins have put in the way, they feel a pain so acute, that if they were capable of death, they could not live a moment. So that, as St. Chrysostom says, this pain of the deprivation of God tortures them incomparably more than the pain of sense: 'The flames of a thousand hells together could not inflict such torments as the pain of loss by itself.' So that those holy souls would rather suffer every other possible torture than be deprived for a single instant of the union with God for which they long. So St. Thomas says that the pain of purgatory exceeds anything that can be endured in this life: 'The pain of purgatory must exceed all pain of this life.' And Dionysius the Carthusian relates, that a dead person, who had been raised to life by the intercession of St. Jerome, told St. Cyril of Jerusalem that all the torments of this earth are refreshing and delightful when compared with the very least pain of purgatory: If all the torments of the world were compared with the least that can be had in purgatory they would appear comfortable.' And he adds, that if a man had once tried those torments, he would rather suffer all the earthly sorrows that man can endure till the Day of Judgment, than suffer for one day the least pain of purgatory. Hence St. Cyril wrote to St. Augustine: 'That as far as regards the infliction of suffering, these pains are the same as those of hell -- their only difference being that they are not eternal.' Hence we see that the pains of these holy souls are excessive, while, on the other hand, they cannot help themselves; because as Job says: They are in chains and are bound with the cords of poverty (Job 36, 8). They are destined to reign with Christ; but they are withheld from taking possession of their kingdom till the time of their purgation is accomplished. And they cannot help themselves (at least not sufficiently, even according to those theologians who assert that they can by their prayers gain some relief,) to throw off their chains, until they have entirely satisfied the justice of God. This is precisely what a Cistercian monk said to the sacristan of his monastery: 'Help me, I beseech you, with your prayers; for of myself I can obtain nothing.' And this is consistent with the saying of St. Bonaventure: 'Destitution prevents solvency.' That is, those souls are so poor, that they have no means of making satisfaction.

On the other hand, since it is certain, and even of faith, that by our suffrages, and chiefly by our prayers, as particularly recommended and practiced by the Church, we can relieve those holy souls, I do not know how to excuse that man from sin who neglects to give them some assistance, at least by his prayers. If a sense of duty will not persuade us to succour them, let us think of the pleasure it will give Jesus Christ to see us endeavouring to deliver his beloved spouses from prison, in order that he may have them with him in paradise. Let us think of the store of merit which we can lay up by practicing this great act of charity; let us think, too, that those souls are not ungrateful, and will never forget the great benefit we do them in relieving them of their pains, and in obtaining for them, by our prayers, anticipation of their entrance into glory; so that when they are there they will never neglect to pray for us. And if God promises mercy to him who practices mercy towards his neighbour -- Blessed are the merciful for they shall obtain mercy (Mt. 5, 7) -- he may reasonably expect to be saved who remembers to assist those souls so afflicted, and yet so dear to God. Jonathan, after having saved the Hebrews from ruin by a victory over their enemies, was condemned to death by his father Saul for having tasted some honey against his express commands; but the people came before the king, and said, Shall Jonathan then die, who hath wrought this great salvation in Israel? (I Samuel 14,45). So may we expect that if any of us ever obtains, by his prayers, the liberation of a soul from purgatory, that soul will say to God: 'Lord, suffer not him who has delivered me from my torments to be lost.' And if Saul spared Jonathan's life at the request of his people, God will not refuse the salvation of a Christian to the prayers of a soul which is his own spouse. Moreover, St. Augustine says that God will cause those who in this life have most succoured those holy souls, when they come to purgatory themselves, to be most succoured by others. l may here observe that, in practice, one of the best suffrages is to hear Mass for them, and during the Holy Sacrifice to recommend them to God by the merits and passion of Jesus Christ. The following form may be used: 'Eternal Father, I offer you this Sacrifice of the Body and Blood of Jesus Christ, with all the pains which he suffered in his life and death; and by his passion I recommend to you the souls in purgatory, and especially that of...'etc. And it is a very charitable act to recommend, at the same time, the souls of all those who are at the point of death.

Other Books From Christ the King Library

Christ the King Library is dedicated to preserving traditional Catholic books and has preserved over a thousand of these classic books.

You may be interested in the following:

Writings of Saint Louis de Montfort, which includes The Secret of the Rosary, The Secret of Mary, Friends of the Cross and Love of Eternal Wisdom

Shorter Writings of Saint Alphonsus, which includes How to Converse Familiarly With God, The Methods of Conversing Continually and Familiarly With God, Uniformity With God's Will and What Will Hell Be Like.

The Art of Dying Well by Saint Robert Bellarmine. Saint Robert Bellarmine also wrote Eternal Happiness and The Seven Words Spoken by Christ on the Cross.

Www.ChristtheKingLibrary.com

Made in United States
Orlando, FL
12 February 2024

43485219R00020